CLiCK

GEORGE SULLIVAN

CLICK CLICK CLICK!
PHOTOGRAPHY
FOR CHILDREN

PRESTEL

Munich · London · New York

CONTENTS

Adams (1941)

[**Create your own camera!**]

WHAT IS A PHOTOGRAPH?

A photograph, simply stated, is a picture made by a camera. How is a photograph created? It's an almost magical process. Light rays from the subject being photographed pass through the lens to be captured on the camera's recording surface. In digital cameras, images are recorded electronically and stored on a memory chip or card. Cameras of the 20th century used photographic film as a recording surface.

To better understand the basic principles of photography, examine what is known as a **pinhole camera**. This device consists of a closed box in the front of which a small hole - a lens - has been created. When you point the lens at a subject, light passing through the hole forms an image of the subject on the side opposite.

The pinhole camera is also known as a **camera obscura**. Camera is Latin for the word "room," obscura means "dark." The camera body is a dark room.

Knowledge of the camera obscura has been traced back to ancient times. The Chinese philosopher Mo Ti described such a device in the 5th century BC. In the centuries that followed, scholars and philosophers occasionally made mention of the camera obscura. Italian artist and inventor Leonardo da Vinci wrote the first detailed description of the device in about 1485. During the early decades of the 1800s, the camera obscura led to the invention of the film camera.

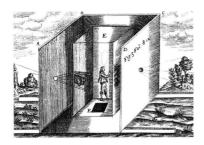

During the mid-1600s, some artists created camera obscuras by building a dark room with lenses and mirrors. Light from the subject being "photographed" produced an image on one of the room's walls. This image could then be traced onto paper by the artist, helping to create a lifelike drawing or painting.

It's not difficult to construct a workable pinhole camera. You need, first of all, a closed box. It can be a box of almost any size—a pillbox, matchbox, shoebox, or cylinder-shaped cereal box. Spray paint the inside with black paint. This prevents reflected light from ruining your photograph.

In one end of the box, cut a hole about the size of a dime. Take a 1 ½-inch square of aluminum foil and make a pinhole in the exact center of it. Use a sewing needle to make the hole. Using black masking tape, tape the square of aluminum foil over the dime-shaped hole you created earlier.

For a shutter,* make a flap over the pinhole out of a short strip of black tape and a square of dark paper. The black tape serves as the flap's hinge. Whenever you're not taking a picture, use a second piece of tape to tightly close the shutter.

You must load your camera in the dark or by using a photography safelight. Cut a piece of black-and-white photographic paper to match in size the inside end of the box opposite the pinhole "lens." On the back of the paper, place a strip of double-sided tape. Mount the paper on the inside end of the box.

To take a photograph, place the camera on a table, chair, or other firm support. Point the lens toward the object you're photographing. Without moving the camera, lift the black flap to uncover the pinhole. Exposure* time can last up to a few minutes. You may have to experiment with the size of the pinhole and the amount of exposure time before you get good results.

Be sure to focus on a stationary object — a fire hydrant, tree, or building — when taking the picture. **Pinhole cameras aren't meant for action shots.**

To unload the paper, again use a dark room. You'll then need to use special chemicals to make the images appear and become permanent. If you don't have these chemicals, you can check with a professional photographer for help.

ABOVE Engraving of a camera obscura, by German scientist Athanasius Kircher (1646)

[How do modern cameras work?]
DIGITAL VERSUS FILM

You can use a **digital camera** or **film camera** to do the things you read about in this book. But digital cameras offer a number of advantages over film.

Digital images are captured on the camera's recording surface by light-sensitive "pixels,*" which is short for "picture elements." Each digital photograph is made up of millions of pixels. Like the pieces of a jigsaw puzzle, each pixel holds a piece of the picture.

The number of pictures that you can take with a digital camera is virtually unlimited. The digital camera's LCD (for liquid crystal display) monitor displays the images stored in your camera and permits you to delete any that are unwanted. So don't hesitate to take a lot of photos. Erase the bad ones; keep the best.

Is this a photograph? Millions of digital photographs appear on the Internet. The American artist Robert Silvers has made his own "photos" from such images. His portrait of Pope John Paul II may look like a photograph. But if you examine it closely, you'll see it's actually a montage made of thousands of tiny digitized photos of churches.

And with a digital camera, you can upload your photographs to your computer, which means that you can email them to friends or relatives. You can also edit your pictures with easily available software, some of which is free. Digital cameras keep getting better and more sophisticated. But it's not likely you will need one that boasts up-to-the-minute technology. Simply choose a camera that matches your needs.

[The camera's role in events that changed humankind ...]

PHOTOS THAT MADE HISTORY

A photograph can be a powerful and influential tool. It can capture a special moment as history is being made. It can arouse emotions and affect the way people think and act. For example, photographs that depict poverty or racism can help promote social changes. Elections can be influenced and government leaders stirred. This section profiles eight historic and power-filled photographs, images that made things happen.

Who invented photography?

It's not easy to say.

Louis Daguerre, a French stage designer and painter, often gets the credit. In 1837, Daguerre perfected the daguerreotype, which is hailed as the first popular method of photography. In a daguerreotype, a delicate, wonderfully detailed image is captured on a silver-coated surface that has been treated with the chemical iodine. During the 1840s and 1850s, daguerreotype portraits were enormously popular, especially in the United States.

RIGHT The first known permanent photograph from nature, by Joseph Nicephore Niepce (1826)

William Henry Fox Talbot, a wealthy young Englishman, has also been described as photography's inventor. In 1839, after years of experimentation, Talbot announced the first successful photographic process that involved the concept of a negative from which any number of positive prints could be made. (The daguerreotype was a one-of-a-kind image; it produced no negative.) Talbot's invention led to the photographic processes of the 19th and 20th centuries.

Niepce's photograph, taken from the upper story of the family's country home, pictures a loft window of the home, a pear tree, the slanted roof of the barn, and the long roof of the bake house behind it.

But before Talbot, before Daguerre, a French inventor named **Joseph Nicephore Niepce** produced what was at the time a startling breakthrough in the visual arts. In the summer of 1826, Niepce was continuing his experiments in photography at his family's country home in Saint-Loup-de-Varennes in eastern France. One morning he set up a camera obscura in the third floor workroom. Opposite the lens, which he focused through an open window facing a sunlit scene, he placed a polished pewter plate, which he had coated with a tar-like substance known as bitumen of Judea. After an exposure of eight hours, he removed the plate and washed it with a mixture of lavender and white petroleum. A picture of the scene taken through the window slowly became visible.

Niepce formed a partnership with Daguerre in 1829. He died in 1833. When Daguerre made a public announcement of the daguerreotype process in 1839, Niepce's contribution was all but blotted out.

In a sense, photography had three inventors — Daguerre, Talbot, and Niepce. But Niepce, by producing the world's earliest known permanent photograph from nature, was the first. His work stands as the foundation for the process of photography that has so dramatically changed the world for nearly two centuries.

FIRST PHOTOGRAPHED PERSON

Taken by photographic pioneer Louis Daguerre in 1838, a year before photography was announced to the public, this image was a marvel of the time. It required an exposure* of about ten minutes.

Daguerre titled the picture "View of Boulevard du Temple, Paris." What makes the picture something more than an admirable view of an empty city street are the figures in the foreground. You can see a man standing with one leg raised, while before him sits a boy shining his shoes. Photo historians thus look upon the image as the **first photograph of a person**.

It is not likely that Daguerre thought out this scene in advance. In the ten minutes it took to make the exposure, things happened. The picture was unplanned, no doubt even undreamed of. It is indeed history's first picture of a person. It also might be called photography's first snapshot.

ABOVE *"View of the Boulevard du Temple, Paris,"* by Louis Daguerre (1838)

STOPPING TIME

On a warm, sunlit morning in mid-June 1878, a crowd of newspapermen and racing enthusiasts gathered beside the race course at the Palo Alto, California, stables owned by American business tycoon Leland Stanford. They were there to witness an unusual experiment. Conducted by British-born photographer **Eadweard Muybridge**, the demonstration was meant to determine whether all four hooves of a running horse were ever off the ground all at once. Stanford had bet they were.

In a low, whitewashed building on one side of the track, twelve bulky cameras had been "lined up," said one account, "like cannons in a galleon." A tall screen of white cloth had been erected on the other side of the track to provide contrast.

On a signal from Muybridge, a uniformed driver climbed into a lightweight two-wheeled cart called a sulky. Taking the reins, he urged one of Stanford's prize trotting horses down the track at a gallop. Buried in the track were twelve wires, each connected to a different camera. When the sulky's wheels rolled over a wire, they completed an electrical circuit, tripping the shutter* of the camera to which it was linked. Each shot was taken in less than half a second. Muybridge quickly developed the camera's glass plates and laid them out for the guests to admire. The remarkable photographic sequence proved beyond the slightest doubt that a galloping horse lifts all four feet simultaneously, and Stanford collected his wager.

As a **"photographic artist,"** the title he gave himself, Muybridge was the first to develop a system for taking a series of still photographs of a body in motion; he made time stand still. Muybridge's groundbreaking sequence photographs still influence visual artists today. They depict men, women, wrestlers, boxers, racehorses, and camels — all frozen in time in the act of walking, running, jumping, dancing, galloping, and somersaulting.

Stanford wasn't the only beneficiary that day. Muybridge's images stunned the art world by exposing glaring errors in countless horse paintings and sculptures, earning him international renown as both a photographer and scientist. But Muybridge was no scientist. His motion studies were not conducted according to scientific principles. He duplicated, replaced, and renumbered frames, and some sequences included posed pictures. The pictorially-acceptable final print was what was important to Muybridge, not how it was achieved.

Artists, photographers, and filmmakers continue to utilize his human and animal locomotion studies. Cartoon animators of the present day regularly trace over Muybridge's century old frame-by-frame sequences in producing animated films, a technique known as rotoscoping. Muybridge's scientific vision of capturing motion on film led ultimately to the development of the first motion picture projector. Indeed, Muybridge is often called "The Father of Motion Pictures."

FIRST SNAPSHOTS

Some people advance photography as an art or science with ground-breaking photographs. Others trigger important changes by introducing processes or materials not known before. That's what **George Eastman** did. He invented a new and wholly different film process that changed photography for all time.

Before Eastman's discovery, taking a photograph was hard work. It involved a big, heavy, cumbersome camera; glass plates upon which the image was recorded; and an assortment of chemicals. Each exposure took

CLiCK

Within a short time after the introduction of the Kodak camera, with its dry, flexible film, thousands of Kodaks were sold. In time, practically everyone was taking quick, informal pictures — snapshots. The Kodak not only revolutionized photography, it transformed the nation and the way people document their lives.

several seconds. You had to have special knowledge and training to take a photograph.

George Eastman changed all that. In 1877, Eastman, then a bank clerk, wanted to photograph a piece of land he was thinking of buying. When he purchased one of those huge cameras to take the picture, he was told he would have to pay someone to teach him how to use it. "There must be an easier way," he said. He made up his mind to find it.

He first figured out how to replace the wet-glass plate process with pre-coated glass. The next step was to substitute glass plates with paper film. The film could be cut into narrow strips and wound on a spindle. These advances led directly to another invention of Eastman's, the Kodak camera.

The name Kodak was a made up word. Eastman thought the letter K was "strong and incisive." He tried out other letters to follow the K and eventually ended up with "Kodak."

The **Kodak camera** was a photographer's dream come true. As many as a hundred exposures could be made with a single roll of film. Users of the camera sent their exposed rolls to Kodak's Rochester, New York, headquarters for developing.

CLiCK

ABOVE **A baby elephant at the zoo, a Kodak snapshot from about 1890**

FIRST FLIGHT

December 17, 1903, near Kitty Hawk, North Carolina, was clear and very cold, with a blustery wind out of the north. On that day, **Orville and Wilbur Wright** made aviation history. Orville was at the controls of their rickety aircraft, powered by a clattering gasoline engine, as it moved slowly down a wooden track and lifted shakily into the air. It stayed up for 12 seconds. It traveled 120 feet.

!

John Daniels' photograph of the Wright Brothers' historic flight near Kitty Hawk, North Carolina, on December 17, 1903. Orville Wright is at the plane's controls; Wilbur runs beside the aircraft.

But that modest achievement was a landmark event in aviation history. It was the **first ever successful flight** of a heavier-than-air vehicle.

Several members of the nearby Kill Devil Hills Life-Saving station witnessed the flight. These men helped rescue victims of shipwrecks, and they cheered as the fragile-bodied aircraft climbed into the air. John Daniels, one member of the group, played a key role that day.

In the minutes before the flight, with the aircraft poised for takeoff, its engine rattling, its two propellers twirling, Wilbur Wright hurriedly set up a glass-plate box camera on a tripod. He carefully pointed the lens toward the end of the rail planted in the beach sand. Then he asked Daniels to serve as the event photographer, even though Daniels had never taken a picture in his life. Wilbur showed Daniels how to squeeze the rubber bulb that would trip the camera's shutter.* He told him to wait for the precise moment that the aircraft lifted into the air.

Daniels followed instructions perfectly. His photograph captures the historic moment when the Wright aircraft took flight.

It was the only photograph that Daniels took in his lifetime. But it is, arguably, the most important aviation photograph of all time.

FIRST ATOMIC EXPLOSION

In the early morning darkness of July 16, 1945, on an isolated stretch of desert at a government location about 35 miles southeast of Socorro, New Mexico, the unimaginable destructive powers of the atom were fully recognized for the first time. The test that took place that morning was the end result of three years of planning and development on the part of the Manhattan Project, the scientific team that was headquartered at the

Alamogordo Bombing and Gunnery Range near Los Alamos, New Mexico. "Trinity" was the code name for the test, but workers referred to the weapon as "The Gadget."

The photo showed for the first time the enormous mushroom cloud of a **nuclear explosion**. Destruction and radioactive debris spread outward from the base of the cloud. Heat, light, and gale-like winds also radiated from the site. The shock wave was felt for more than a hundred miles.

One of the first photos of a nuclear explosion, taken over the New Mexican desert on July 16, 1945.

World War II was raging at the time in the Pacific. Even before Trinity, a second bomb was being readied by the United States for an attack against the Japanese. On August 6, 1945, three weeks after the Trinity test, that bomb was dropped on the city of Hiroshima.

EARTHRISE

At 6:31 a.m. on Saturday, December 21, 1968, the 360-foot Saturn V, the tallest, most powerful **rocket** ever built, blasted astronauts Frank Borman, Bill Anders, and Jim Lovell into space. The sound at liftoff assaulted people's eardrums. "The Earth shakes, cars rattle, and vibrations beat in the chest," is the way author Anne Morrow Lindbergh put it.

ABOVE **Explosion of the Trinity atomic bomb, July 16, 1945**

The rocket performed without mishap, putting their **Apollo 8** space capsule safely into orbit. Lovell then fired the launcher's third stage to send their spacecraft racing on its three-day journey to the moon.

Early on Christmas Eve, Apollo 8 reached its destination and prepared to go into orbit around the moon. Once the spacecraft was in position behind the moon, communication with Earth went silent. Around the world, nearly a billion people in sixty-four countries waited ten anxiety-filled minutes before contact resumed.

"It's an historic moment," said a spokesperson for the National Aeronautics and Space Administration (NASA). "For the first time men are literally out of this world, under the influence of another celestial body ..."

For its first three revolutions, the astronauts kept the windows of the spacecraft pointing downward toward the surface of the moon so they could film the craters and mountains below. But for the fourth orbit, Borman rolled the spacecraft so as to position the windows toward the horizon.

Suddenly Borman noticed a blue-and-white fuzzy blob edging up from behind the moon's sharp gray horizon line. He knew what he was seeing: the **planet Earth**, then a quarter of a million miles away, was rising from behind the moon.

"Oh, my God," he cried out. "Look at that picture over there! Here's the earth coming up!" He stared in wonder. "Wow, is that pretty!"

Borman was quick to react. In the weightless atmosphere of the spaceship, a camera that Anders had been using floated by. Borman grabbed it and quickly snapped a picture. "Hey, don't take that," Anders joked. "It's not scheduled." They all laughed.

Borman handed the camera to Anders, who supervised the taking of photographs. He realized that the camera was loaded with black-and-white film. "Hand me that roll of color quick," he said to Lovell, who was close to

the storage locker. Anders loaded the film into the camera and then the two men jostled for position at the window.

By this time, the Earth had risen several degrees above the horizon. The dazzling blue-white ocean gleamed against the jet-black sky. The moon's gray horizon loomed in the foreground.

As Anders framed his shot, Lovell hung over his shoulder. "Oh, that's a beautiful shot," he said. He asked Anders to take a number of pictures using different exposures.

Anders nodded. "I did," he said.

At that moment, the sun on Earth was setting along the terminator, the dividing line between the dark side and bright side of the moon. In Anders' picture, the terminator runs through Africa, with light above it and darkness below.

The three men stared at the planet as it climbed slowly in the sky. They had become **the first humans to witness an earthrise**.

Six days after leaving Earth, the Apollo 8 mission ended when the space-craft splashed down in the Pacific Ocean near Hawaii. It didn't take long for Anders' picture to be circulated around the world and become one the most reproduced images in history. A striking reminder of how vulnerable the Earth is, the photo quickly became revered by the movement to protect the earth and its resources.

"There are basically two messages that come to me," Anders said of the picture. "One of them is that the planet is quite fragile. It reminded me of a Christmas tree ornament."

"But the other message is that the Earth is really small. We're not the center of the universe. We're way out in left field on a tiny dust mote, but it is our home and we have to take care of it."

RED PLANET

For centuries, scientists wondered what **Mars**, the fourth planet from the sun in the solar system, was really like. Was there water there? Could the planet be covered with vegetation? Might it be inhabited by humans?

The atmosphere of Mars, taken in 1976 during the Viking 1 mission. On the left, you can see the Galle crater, which looks like a smiley face.

Today, the answers to those questions are well known. Mars is a frozen desert. Its huge volcanoes are now silent, and its polar ice caps resemble those on Earth. But there is no human life, no vegetation.

The fact that Mars is an alien world of sterile soil and weird salmon-colored sky was first revealed by the **Viking 1 and 2** space missions. Landers from these two spacecraft were the first to conduct biological tests for life on the planet. And on July 20, 1976, the Viking 1 lander sent the **first color images** taken on the planet's surface back to Earth.

This feat was accomplished thanks to digital imagery, which was in its development stage at the time. A film camera would have been useless. The exposed film would have had to be brought back to Earth for development, and Viking landers I and 2 were not returning.

Other images taken on Mars show surface colors similar to those on Earth, and blue sky. Several hours after the first transmissions, the National Aeronautics and Space Agency (NASA) released an update with photos that featured reddish soil and an orange sky. Although this is the popular idea of what the planet looks like, some scientists believe the original colors are closer to reality. Undoubtedly, future space probes will provide more accurate images of Mars, and these will help to settle the debate.

CLICK

[**The men and women who taught us new ways to see the world ...**]

MASTER PHOTOGRAPHERS

There might be as many as a hundred or so men and women of the past century-and-a-half that can be called master photographers. They are, or were, the profession's very best. While they reflect a wide range of specialties, each exhibited many of the same qualities: ambition, a clear motive, technical expertise, creativity, and an eye for detail. This section profiles eleven of these highly skilled artists.

FELIX NADAR

Felix Nadar, whose real name was Gaspard-Felix Tornachon, spent most of his life in Paris. Not only was he a master of photography, he was also a **master of publicity**. He became famous for photographing celebrities, and he once built his own air balloon so he could take what were history's first aerial photographs.

BORN
April 5, 1820
BIRTHPLACE
Paris, France
DIED
March 21, 1910

Nadar photographed actors, political leaders, musicians, and artists. His portrait photos were among the first to explore and reveal the personality of each of his subjects—as painted portraits had long done. When he photographed the French actress Sarah Bernhardt, he captured her dramatic nature. When he pictured **Gioachino Rossini**, he brought to light the Italian composer's humorous side. In so doing, Nadar helped to create the profession of artist-photographer.

EUGÈNE ATGET

Born outside the French city of Bordeaux, Atget settled in Paris in the 1890s. Toward the end of the decade, he began to compile a comprehensive visual record of the city. Hauling his heavy, bulky, large-format view camera about the **Paris streets**, he photographed buildings, storefronts, parks, gardens, people, and the bridges and quays of the river Seine. These photographs were not mere documentary images. Atget knew exactly what to do with focus, lighting, and composition,* and he had a special talent for recording detail. Much of his work conformed to the standards of art.

BORN
February 12, 1857
BIRTHPLACE
Bordeaux, France
DIED
August 4, 1927

Photographer Berenice Abbott, well known for her striking images of New York City, and who helped preserve Atget's work, wrote of him: "He was an urbanist historian, a Balzac of the camera, from whose work we can weave a large tapestry of French civilization."

ANSEL ADAMS

BORN
February 24, 1902
BIRTHPLACE
San Francisco
DIED
April 22, 1984

Well before the end of his long life, Ansel Adams had become an **American icon**, widely hailed as much for his breathtaking black-and-white photos of Yosemite Valley in California as for his zealous support of environmental movements and their goals. The unending flow of posters, calendars, books, and computer screen-savers derived from his photos is clear evidence as to the legendary status that he and his work attained.

Though music was an early passion of Adams', and he was trained as a concert pianist, he decided in 1930 that his calling was photography, and the natural landscapes of Yosemite were to be his specialty. His earliest work was done in the soft focus and rich printing that were the hallmarks of pictorialism, the style of photography popular at the time. But before long, Adams came to be deeply influenced by more forward-thinking American photographers, such as Edward Weston, Alfred Steigltz, and, especially, Paul Strand. As a result, Adams' majestic landscapes began to reflect the sharp focus and stirring detail of modernism.

In Adams' photograph "The Tetons — Snake River," the river guides the eye, easing its way through the small foothills to the tall mountains in the back-ground. The upper third of the picture is given over to cloud-brushed sky. To boost the **dramatic quality** of the picture, Adams improved the contrast* by means of what is called the zone system. He adjusted the tonal quality of each of the various subjects within a photograph so as to boost the pic-ture's clarity and depth. A three-dimensional quality was the result.

Adams won praise not only for his photographs but also for his contri-butions as a teacher and author. He ran workshops in Yosemite Valley on the basics of photography and published a series of books on that topic. He lectured at colleges along the Pacific Coast and at the Museum of Modern Art in New York, where he helped found the department of photography.

By the end of his career, Adams ranked as the best-known photographer in the United States. His work had been published in more than thirty-five books and portfolios. Photographs of his had been seen in hundreds of exhibitions. In 1980, he was awarded the Medal of Freedom, America's highest civilian honor. In 1985, on the first anniversary of his passing, an 11,900-foot Yosemite peak was officially named Mount Ansel Adams in his honor.

In Wyoming in 1941, Adams produced one of his most majestic photos titled "The Tetons — Snake River." The Tetons, or the Grand Tetons, to use the full name, is a towering mountain range found just south of Yellowstone in Jackson Hole, Wyoming. The Snake River begins in the Rocky Mountains and winds its way through America's Pacific Northwest.

HENRI CARTIER-BRESSON

Photojournalists, documentary photographers, and street photographers the world over owe a debt of gratitude to Henri Cartier-Bresson. His ability to see a fleeting image and capture it on film in the blink of an eye helped to create a new standard in the world of photography. His best photographs are looked upon as **prime examples of 20th century art**.

BORN
August 22, 1908
BIRTHPLACE
Chanteloupe, France
DIED
August 3, 2004

Cartier-Besson was influenced by a new and exciting German school of design called the Bauhaus. In the late 1920's, Bauhaus teachers were showing their students how to discard the fussy ideas of the past in favor of clear, concise documentary images. This style would be adopted by Cartier-Bresson.

Henri also benefited from technical progress in photography. In 1925, the **Leica**, the first practical 35mm camera, not much bigger than today's point-and-shoot cameras, was introduced at the Leipzig Spring Fair in Leipzig, Germany. The Leica opened up a new world for photographers. Now they could make pictures quickly and easily.

It wasn't until the early 1930s that Cartier-Bresson, returning to France from a trip to Africa, took up photography. It was at that time that he probably acquired his first Leica.

"I prowled the streets all day, feeling very strung-up and ready to pounce, determined to 'trap' life, to preserve the act of living," he once recalled. "Above all, I craved to seize the whole essence in the confines of one single photograph, of some situation that was rolling before my eyes."

CLiCK

CLiCK

CLiCK

CLiCK

Sharp-eyed and with lightning reflexes, Cartier-Bresson captured over and over what he called the "decisive moment," that split second when reality blends with perfect composition.

Cartier-Bresson was never without his Leica. He equipped the camera with a 50mm lens that he used almost exclusively. He used no tripod, flash, flood-lights, reflectors, or other gear common among professional photographers.

Henri believed that the picture he composed in the viewfinder* was almost sacred. There was to be no cropping or other darkroom tinkering. The idea of using a computer program to doctor an image would have sickened him. Not only did he insist that his prints not be cropped, he ordered that each print include the first millimeter of unexposed clear negative surround-ing the image. This resulted, after printing, in a slim black border around the picture.

Henri had no wish to develop his film or make his own prints. "I've never been interested in the process of photography, never, never," he once said. "For me, photography with a small camera like the Leica is an instant drawing."

Cartier-Bresson often sought to make himself unseeable. There are very few photographs of Henri himself. During ceremonies at Oxford Univer-sity in 1975, when he was awarded an honorary degree, Henri held a paper in front of his face to avoid being snapped. He seldom granted interviews.

The celebrated artist, Edgar Degas, once said: "It's wonderful to be famous as long as you can remain unknown." Cartier-Bresson loved that remark. He liked nothing better than to mix with people on crowded streets and not be recognized. His **anonymity** was a treasured asset.

In an interview with *Newsweek* magazine toward the end of his life, Cartier-Bresson remarked, **"Anyone with a camera is a photographer."** His wife, who was present, objected loudly. Whatever Cartier-Bresson did in capturing a photograph's decisive moment may have come easily to him, but to almost every other person who has wielded a camera it remains an elusive skill.

CLICK

CLICK

WALKER EVANS

BORN
November 3, 1903
BIRTHPLACE
St. Louis, Missouri
DIED
April 10, 1975

From 1935 to 1943, a group of about twenty photographers who worked for the United States federal government produced the nation's most striking images of the **Great Depression**, a dismal period in American history caused by a collapse in the economy. It began in 1929 and lasted through most of the 1930s. These men and women were assigned to create a pictorial record of the hard times being experienced by Americans living in rural areas. Their photographs would be a way of winning support for the federal government's economic and social programs that were meant to relieve the problems.

What is perhaps Walker Evans' most productive period as a photographer came during the eighteen months he was employed by a branch of the federal government. This branch was called the photographic unit of the Farm Security Administration, the FSA. During this time, Evans photographed poverty-stricken families, the interiors of their homes, country schoolhouses, grocery stores, and garages. He also captured broken-down cars and trucks, billboards, hand-lattered signs, and other artifacts of people's daily lives.

Evans' pictures had great clarity, simplicity, and directness. But they showed no emotional involvement on his part. He saw no reason to make his own feelings self-evident.

His subjects speak for themselves. A photo dating to 1936, which depicts a street scene in Georgia, is evidence.

CLICK

A billboard advertising the Hollywood film "Love Before Breakfast," featuring Carol Lombard, a popular actress of the time, dominates this photo of a street scene in Atlanta, Georgia. It appears directly in front of a pair of rundown clapboard houses. Simply, clearly, Evans had put Hollywood's world of make believe in **sharp contrast with the realities of everyday life. No caption is necessary.**

In 1938, the year he left the FSA, Evans received an important honor. The Museum of Modern Art in New York City honored Evans with a solo exhibition, the first one the museum had ever dedicated to one photographer.

ABOVE **A street scene in Atlanta, Georgia, by Walker Evans (1936)**

Also in 1938, Evans embarked on a new project, photographing New York City subway riders without any of them realizing it. He hung a small camera about his neck and concealed it with his coat. The lens poked out through a buttonhole. Evans snapped each picture by means of a long cable that wormed its way through his sleeve to the shutter* release in his hand.

During World War II, Evans photographed workers and industry, with leading magazines of the day as his clients. Beginning in 1945, he was a staff photographer for *Fortune* magazine, a position he held for twenty years.

Walker Evans had a powerful influence on major documentary photographers that followed him, including Robert Frank and Lee Friedlander. The objects he photographed were seldom considered suitable subject matter until he turned his camera on them.

Although he photographed such ordinary subjects as barbershops and junkyards, Evans never doubted he was an artist. "When I first made photographs, they were too plain to be considered art, and I wasn't considered an artist," he said. "I didn't get any attention at all. The people who looked at my work thought, well, that's just a snapshot of the backyard. Privately I knew otherwise and through stubbornness stayed with it."

LEWIS HINE

BORN
September 26, 1874
BIRTHPLACE
Oshkosh,
Wisconsin
DIED
November 3, 1940

CLiCK

CLiCK

CLiCK

"Photography can light up darkness and expose ignorance," said Lewis Hine. Lewis Hine's cameras did just that. Trained as a sociologist and journalist, **Hine made photographs that documented the exploitation of children** during the early 20th century. They also helped promote the passage of labor laws in the United States to protect young workers.

ABOVE "A Little Spinner in the Mollahan Mills, Newberry, S.C.," by Lewis Hine (1908)

Child labor was cheap labor in the America of 1900. A young worker in a North Carolina cotton mill was paid 48 cents a day for tending mill machinery. Asked how old she was, she said, "I don't remember." Then she added, "I'm not old enough to work, but do just the same." Of the mill's fifty employees, ten were children.

Hine made no effort to magnify the problem, even though his critics said his photographs were "not shocking enough." Hine believed that people would be more likely to support child labor legislation if photographers were entirely honest in communicating the realities of children's working conditions.

Hine's camera was big and heavy and hard to lug around. Photographers were sometimes hired for their physical strength rather than their talent.

Indoor photographs of the time were an adventure. They required the use of magnesium flash powder. The necessary explosion of the powder not only produced a blinding amount of light but also a roomful of smelly smoke. The people that Hine photographed were often caught with their mouths open and their eyes blinking. Singed hair and eyebrows were not unknown.

In 1907, Hine began working for the National Child Labor Committee (NCLC), an organization dedicated to abolishing all child labor. Over the next several years, using the same camera he had used for his Ellis Island pictures, Hine traveled to dangerous coal mines in Pennsylvania, textile mills in New England, and seafood packing plants along the Gulf Coast. He photographed child newspaper sellers, cigar rollers, and basket weavers.

Hine was careful to record data about the children he photographed. He noted the height, age, and the general health and appearance of each.

A breakthrough came in 1916 when the U.S. government passed legislation that restricted the employment of children fourteen and under in factories and shops. An official of the NCLC declared, "The work Hine did for this reform was more responsible than all other efforts in bringing this need to public attention." In later years, the government would pass laws restricting many other forms of child labor.

DOROTHEA LANGE

BORN
May 26, 1895
BIRTHPLACE
Hoboken,
New Jersey
DIED
October 11, 1965

A specialist in portraits and documentary photography, Dorothea Lange is best known for her searing photos taken for the Farm Security Administration during the 1930s. Her iconic images of sharecroppers, displaced farm families, and migrant workers earned her recognition as a **documentary photographer** without equal.

Lange's portrait titled **"Migrant Mother"** is her most famous. It was taken in Nipomo, California, at a pea pickers camp. The workers had no work because the pea crop was frozen. They were stranded. In an interview in 1960, Lange talked about the woman: "She told me her age, that she was 32. She said that they had been living on frozen vegetables from the surrounding fields, and birds that the children killed. She had just sold the tires from her car to buy food. There she sat in that lean-to tent with her children huddled around her, and seemed to know that my pictures might help her, and so she helped me."

Lange also won wide acclaim for her work documenting Japanese-American families who were forced by the United States government to leave their homes and live in relocation camps during World War II. These people were charged with no crime; they were denied any opportunity to appeal. The tarpaper-covered barracks in which they lived had no cooking or plumbing facilities, and only cots for beds. Lange's photographs revealed the hardships that these Japanese-Americans suffered, but the government did not allow her images to be seen for many years.

In 1972, the Whitney Museum in New York City offered 27 of these photographs in an exhibition that documented the period of Japanese-American internment camps. Lange's photos are available today on the website of the Still Pictures Branch of the U.S. National Archives.

GORDON PARKS

BORN
November 30, 1912
BIRTHPLACE
Fort Scott, Kansas
DIED
March 7, 2006

A high school dropout who became an **award-winning photographer**, Gordon Parks often used his camera to chronicle the black experience in America. Parks was also a poet, novelist, journalist, musician, and film director.

"I didn't set out to do all that I did," Parks told an interviewer. "All the things I did were done because of fear of failure."

Through his determination and skill, Parks became the first black photographer to work for the wildly popular *Life*, the first all-photograph news magazine, and *Vogue*, the preeminent fashion magazine. He was also the first African-American to work for U.S. government agencies called the Office of War Information and the Farm Security Administation (FSA).

With the FSA, Parks wielded the camera almost as if it were an instrument of war. He sought to expose and confront examples of intolerance. "I had known poverty first hand," Parks said, "but here I learned how to fight its evil — along with the evil of racism — with a camera."

During his period as a trainee at the FSA, Parks took one of his most meaningful photographs. It is a **portrait of Mrs. Ella Watson**, a black woman who cleaned offices at the FSA.

In this famous image, Parks posed Mrs. Watson staring straight into the lens. With a mop in one handand a broom in the other, she stood in front of a big American flag on the wall. The photo suggested that American prosperity, symbolized by the flag, was not enjoyed by most African-Americans, who often suffered from racism and poverty.

Parks showed the photograph to Roy Stryker, his boss. "Well, how do you like it?" he asked.

"You're learning," Stryker said. "You're showing you can involve yourself in other people."

Parks joined *Life* as a staff photographer in 1948. Over the next quarter of a century, he completed over 300 assignments for the magazine. "At first he made his name with fashion, but when he covered racial strife for us, there was no question that he was a black photographer with enormous connections and access to the black community and its leaders," said Philip Kunhardt, Jr., assistant managing editor of the magazine.

Parks went on to become the first African-American to write and direct a Hollywood film — *Shaft* — and was a co-founder of *Essence*, a fashion and beauty magazine for black women.

In 2002, at age 90, Parks received the Jackie Robinson Foundation Lifetime Achievement Award and was also inducted into the International Photography Hall of Fame. These honors recognized how important Parks's photographs were in challenging long-held American racial stereotypes.

YOU AND YOUR CAMERA

BECOMING A PHOTOGRAPHER

[**Get acquainted with your camera.**]

PICTURE PERFECT

Taking pictures with a digital camera may seem to be a cinch. You get the image you want in the viewfinder, and then snap away. It seems easy. But taking a perfectly focused, perfectly exposed photo of **exceptional quality** is another matter. It's a learning experience.

At the beginning, take time to master the basic functions of your camera, which are explained in detail in the instruction manual. Don't leave home without that little booklet.

For most of the pictures you take, you'll want to keep your camera level. When taking a shot, get in the habit of looking for a level horizontal surface you can use as a guide. Maybe it's the flat roof of a building. Sometimes you can use the horizon as your point of reference, as when you're taking a sunset or sunrise. And there's always the **horizontal lines** of the camera's LCD monitor.

To avoid blurred photos, you must keep the camera steady. Always grasp it with both hands.

Keeping your elbows close to your body also helps in holding the camera still. You can even try leaning against something solid, a wall or a fence post, for instance, for greater stability.

Camera shake can also be overcome by using a **tripod**. Don't think of the tripod solely as a professional's tool. It's a necessary piece of equipment. Using one helps to assure the sharpest possible images.

If a tripod doesn't appeal to you, consider a monopod, a single-legged camera support. Not only does the monopod offer stability, it also provides mobility. Its several sections of aluminum tubing slide together like a telescope to about the size of a Coke bottle. It fits easily into a backpack or camera bag.

Just as you should use both hands when holding the camera, you should **use both eyes** when looking through the viewfinder.* It's natural to keep one eye closed when deciding what you want to appear in your picture. But that limits your field of vision. Suppose you want to photograph a speeding car, for example. It's difficult to follow the car with one eye closed. It takes both eyes to see where the car is heading. Practice looking through the viewfinder with both eyes until it feels natural.

Take time to learn the proper use of the shutter button. In auto-focus, it's a two-step process. First, press the shutter button halfway down to lock in the focus and exposure.* Pause briefly. Then depress the button the rest of the way to take the photo. If you try to hurry the sequence, the resulting photo is likely to be fuzzy because of camera movement.

Whenever you're preparing to take pictures out of doors, take a serious look at the kind of **light** you're going to be working with. While it is generally best to shoot with the sun behind you, keep in mind that indirect light can sometimes make your subject look more attractive. Also, when bright sun is at your back, you may find that your subject is squinting.

Always be aware of which way the **shadows** are falling. Side lighting from shadows can add a dramatic quality to your pictures. Some photographers, in fact, prefer to do most of their outdoor work in the hour before sunset and the hour after sunrise. That's when the shadows are longer and more intense, which can make the resulting images more poignant and meaningful.

The next time you visit a camera shop, you're likely to find that the latest cameras offer a great array of new and exciting features. While you may benefit by acquiring a camera with dazzling bells and whistles, keep in mind that the camera doesn't create the picture. The camera is merely a tool. It's the photographer who is in control.

[**Make photos that move!**]

CAPTURING ACTION

Base stealers in baseball, ball carriers in football, skateboarders, swimmers, gymnasts, snowboarders, and figure skaters have an exciting quality in their movements. It's a real challenge to attempt to portray that movement in your photographs.

One way to assure getting an action-filled photo is by blurring the subject. Blurring is easy because the subject does most of the work. Use a slow shutter speed and follow the subject in your viewfinder.* Stop and snap the picture when you feel the subject's movement will provide a flowing quality to the photo.

Panning is another method of getting an action-filled picture. Panning is the technique of following or tracking a fast-moving subject that will provide a sharp image of the subject against a blurred background.

Suppose you want to take a picture of a friend on a bicycle speeding past you. Prefocus the camera on the particular spot where you expect

CLiCK

CLiCK

!

When it comes to photographing moving images, **Neil Leifer** is one of the greatest of all time. Sports photography is his specialty. His photographs have appeared on more than 200 covers of *Sports Illustrated* and *Time* magazines. A boy wonder in photography, he had his first picture published in *Sports Illustrated* in 1958 when he was 16.

Leifer's pictures conveyed a **feeling of action**. Sometimes this required special preparation. Leifer once got ready to photograph a downhill ski event by taking pictures of freeway automobiles that were whizzing along at 60 miles an hour.

ABOVE   **Gymnast Nadia Comăneci at the 1976 Summer Olympic Games, by Neil Leifer**

CLICK

to take the photo. (You prefocus by pressing the shutter button halfway down.) Follow the subject with a smooth movement of your camera. Snap the picture at the moment the subject passes through the prefocused spot.

Be sure to move the camera at the same speed as the bicycle is traveling. And also be certain to follow through — that is, continue tracking the subject after you've taken the picture.

When you're seeking to take exciting action photos, look beyond the more popular sports. Sledding and snowboarding in the winter; beach volleyball, rope jumping, skateboarding in the summer; even fishing and boating — all offer their own challenges toward capturing action.

[**Capture colors at night.**]

FIREWORKS

Spectacular displays of **light in the sky** are fun to shoot. And working with a camera on an evening of fireworks will give you something to do besides ooing and aahing.

Switch the shooting mode dial to Night mode. (Some cameras even have Fireworks mode.) This will slow the shutter's speed, which means it's a good idea to use a tripod.

You have to be quick on the draw when photographing fireworks, so don't even think about focusing. Prefocus. Set the focal distance at infinity.

Your most fabulous fireworks shots are likely to come at the very end of the evening at the big finale. Be sure to stick around.

CLiCK CLiCK CLiCK

Now here's an explosion of light! Photographer Clive Rose captured the massive fireworks display at the opening ceremonies of the 2008 Olympic Games in Beijing, China. His photo almost makes the stadium look like a huge punchbowl, with a great splash of orange light erupting from it.

[Transforming people and objects in a snap ...]
PLAYING THE ANGLES

Keeping the camera level when shooting is good advice—in most cases. There are times when you can break that rule, however. There are times you can take photos from really **crazy angles**. It's a way of getting variety into your photographs.

Get down low or climb high to get your photo. Crouch with both knees bent. To get really low, lie on your stomach. Low angles can give a photo the feeling of power. High photos put an emphasis on the picture's horizontal and vertical lines.

Experiment:
Go high, shoot; go higher, shoot; go even higher, shoot.
Compare the results and print the best.

!

Diffrent angles

CLiCK

One photographer who loved crazy angles was the Russian artist Alexander Rodchenko. Some of his angles are so extreme, it's hard to tell at first what he's photographing. In 1929, Rodchenko decided to capture a tall radio tower. Because the artist used such a low angle, the tower appears to go upward forever into the sky. The angle also lets you see interesting shapes within the tower.

American Photographer Philippe Halsman was famous for his unusal photos. This is a high-angle shot of trumpeter and singer Louis Armstrong. It was taken in 1966.

!

[Making photos with personality ...]
PEOPLE PORTRAITS

It's been called the **world's most recognizable photograph**. It's Steve McCurry's photograph of an Afghan refugee girl taken in 1984. The image became famous as the cover photograph of the June 1985 issue of National Geographic magazine. It's been frequently used on brochures, posters, and calendars published by Amnesty International, an organization dedicated to prevent human rights abuses.

For more than thirty years, Steve McCurry has photographed troubled areas of the world. He is concerned with the human consequences of war, and his pictures document that concern. "For the portraits I shoot," he says, "I recognize something fascinating about the way my subjects look, be it in their eyes, the way they are dressed, and I feel some connection that grabs my attention."

He calls the change from film to digital technology in cameras "breathtaking." He once recalled that in the days that he used film he "could go through between 800 to 1,000 rolls of film on a single shoot of which only 20 to 25 really exceptional photos would be chosen for use."

In taking a portrait picture with your own digital camera, the first thing to do is switch to Portrait mode. This will help you to achieve an out-of-focus effect in the picture's background. The background then won't be competing for attention with the subject.

Plan your portrait in advance. Do you want the subject sitting? Standing? What about the background? Avoid having clutter behind the subject and keep any distracting objects out of the foreground.

Also avoid having the subject look straight into the lens. Try having the subject's body and head face in different directions. Sometimes getting a

good posed shot can be difficult because the subject gets tense and stiffens up. It's up to you **to get the person to relax**. First, prefocus, and then get into a conversation with the person. Ask about the person's life. Talk about one of the subject's favorite topics. Tell a joke. Eventually, the subject will become less tense.

Elliott Erwitt, the noted documentary photographer, had a trick he used to get portrait subjects to loosen up. He carried a small bicycle horn in his pocket. When someone was sour-faced or stiff, Erwitt would blow his horn. "It's silly," he said, "but it works."

When photographing young children, **add a prop to the shot.** A favorite toy can help relax the child and add interest to the shot.

Good portraits usually result when you and your subject are at the same eye level. If you're taking pictures of your parents or some other adult, you might want to stand on a low stool or chair. In the case of a young child, get down on your knees. If your subject lies on the ground, you should lie on the ground.

There's nothing wrong with portraits that fail to follow what's said in the preceding paragraph. In other words, don't hesitate to break the rules. Get really high and have your subject look up at you. Get down and shoot up. Weird angles can often produce remarkable results.

Try to capture each subject's personality. If your Dad likes to watch football or baseball on television, take his picture in front of the TV. If he loves his car, picture him in the driver's seat. Or perhaps you can travel to your Dad's office for a photo.

Getting a really good portrait can be an uphill struggle. Don't expect to get what you want with just a few exposures. **What's important is that you first connect with the subject.** Once a bond forms (and you keep snapping), you'll get a picture of high quality, satisfying to both you and your subject.

ABOVE Mrs. Norman Guiou as a child, by Yousuf Karsh (1934)

ABOVE "Pastry Cook," by August Sander (1928)

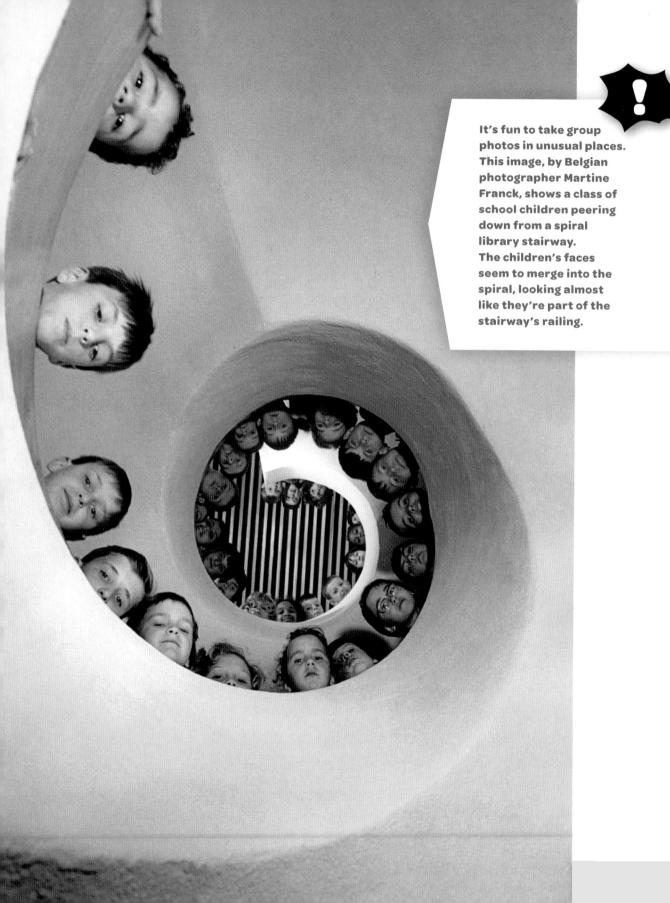

It's fun to take group photos in unusual places. This image, by Belgian photographer Martine Franck, shows a class of school children peering down from a spiral library stairway. The children's faces seem to merge into the spiral, looking almost like they're part of the stairway's railing.

[Clicking with family and friends ...]
GROUP PHOTOS

When taking photos of two or more persons, **be original**. Try to avoid lining up the subjects shoulder to shoulder. That's boring.

Instead of having people stand in a row, put them at different levels. Arrange them in a number of rows, with some people standing, others sitting in chairs, and still others kneeling. Or pose the group on a staircase or on and around a park bench.

When posing a couple, try a front-to-front pose, with the two facing and touching one another. You can also have the two face forward at a slight angle, with one in front of the other.

If the people in a group have a shared interest, your picture should show that they are unified, perhaps by having them touch one another. Or you can pose them with props that represent that interest. For example, if they're members of a field hockey team, pose them with a display of field hockey sticks and masks. Pose bicyclists with a bicycle.

With any group, it's best if everyone wears clothing of the same color tone. A person wearing brighter colors than the others should be placed in the middle of the picture. Tell the group when you're ready to take the photo, and then count out, "One, two, three!" — and snap. If it's a big group, you may have to take several shots before everyone has their eyes open.

[**Get ready for your close-up!**]
SELF-PORTRAIT

Begin your self-portrait by switching to the Portrait icon. This will blur the picture's background, thus assuring it won't be a distraction. Forget about photographing yourself by sticking out your arm and holding the camera when shooting. You'll get a picture but it's likely to look amateurish.

What you want to do is mount your camera on your tripod. If you don't own a tripod, set the camera on a table, counter, or other level and stable surface. Take a test shot or two to be sure you have the focusing and framing right.

Natural light, not flash, is best when you want to take a picture of yourself. Pose indoors beside a window.

> *Experiment:*
> *Move in close to the lens; get farther away. Try smiling; try not smiling. Shoot from on high; shoot from the floor. Try a bunch of goofy shots. Self-portraits can be self-entertainment.*

CLICK

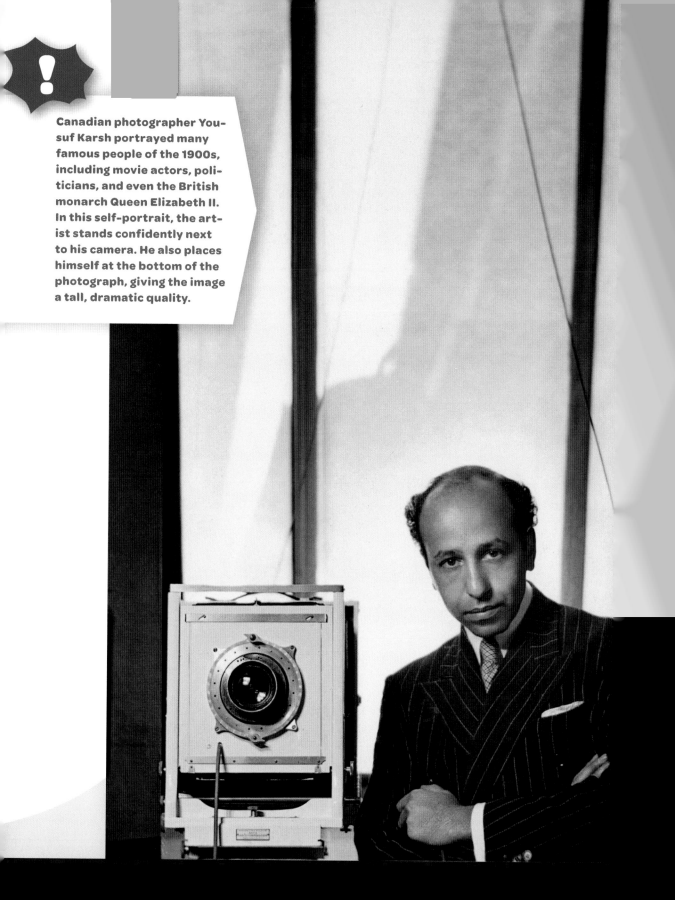

Canadian photographer Yousuf Karsh portrayed many famous people of the 1900s, including movie actors, politicians, and even the British monarch Queen Elizabeth II. In this self-portrait, the artist stands confidently next to his camera. He also places himself at the bottom of the photograph, giving the image a tall, dramatic quality.

[**Photographing your own environment ...**]

LANDSCAPES

Edward Burtynsky, a Canadian photographer and artist, has won worldwide recognition for his grand, colorful landscapes. But don't look for photographs of sunsets, forests, or shorelines from Burtynsky. The landscapes that he photographs are meant to show the **alarming ways in which the planet is being reshaped**. Burtynsky's images depict massive scrap piles, mountains of discarded tires, junked vehicles, the bright orange waste from a nickel mine, and the Gulf of Mexico oil spill in 2010. He has also photographed the Three Gorges Dam in China, perhaps the world's biggest engineering project, and one that has threatened the forced relocation of more than a million people.

Burtynsky's photographs can be breathtaking; they are both **beautiful and horrifying.** In this photo, you can see the orange waste from a nickel mine. The image was taken by Burtynsky in Sudbury, Ontario in 1996.

ABOVE "Nickel Tailings #34," by Edward Burtynsky (1996)

You may not have the global array of subjects that Burtynsky has, but there are likely to be wide expanses of natural scenery nearby that offer the potential for inspiring photographs. Whether you're photographing an inland view or a coastal panorama, it's important to first establish what the best atmospheric and lighting conditions are for your picture. Spend some time at the site. The character of a landscape can change dramatically depending on the time of day and weather conditions. It can also vary with the seasons of the year. Getting the right moment for the photograph is just as important in landscape photography as it is in taking portraits.

ABOVE   **View of the south side of Mt. McKinley in Alaska, USA, National Geographic**

Set your camera to the Landscape mode. This assures a small aperture* opening and, thus, greater depth of field.* Depth of field is the zone of acceptable focus in a photograph. If the nearest in-focus object is 10 feet from the lens and the farthest object in sharp focus is 30 feet away, the image has a depth of field of 20 feet. For landscapes, you want as much depth of field as possible.

The drawback with great depth of field is that the slightest camera movement will result in blur. That's why landscape photography calls for the use of a tripod. If you don't have a tripod, try its cousin, the monopod.

Take your time to walk around the site. **Make some test shots.** Check the way the look of the scene changes as your perspective changes. What's the best angle for the shot? How much sky do you want? Late afternoon and early morning light provide long shadows that help to emphasize depth.

Make a special effort to find an object in the foreground that can be included in the picture. It may be a fence or a dirt road, or a row of bushes, a clump of trees, or a rock formation. Such objects add drama to the photo.

When you shoot, be sure to fill the frame. Every element, from one edge of the scene to the other, is important.

[Portray the animal characters in your family.]

PET PARADE

A 20th-century master of photography, **Elliott Erwitt** loves dogs. His book *Dog Dogs* offers more than 500 dog photos (also horses, pigs, cows, cats, and even people). There are all kinds of dogs in his book. There are dogs on sofas, beaches, park benches, and in dog shows. There are dogs hanging out together. There are dogs jumping in the air out of joy. There are anxious dogs, sorrowful dogs, and disappointed dogs.

In all, the book is further evidence of Erwitt's style and wit.

Erwitt is modest about what he does. "The work I do is terribly simple," he said. "I observe; I try to entertain, but above all I want pictures that are emotional."

!

ABOVE Portrait of dalmatians with glasses, by Elliott Erwitt (2003)

CLiCK

Getting emotion into pet pictures is no easy task. Whether you're taking pictures of a dog or a cat, a ferret or a gecko, it takes patience, persistence, and the ability to snap at that "decisive moment." Take the time to size up the animal before you begin clicking away. Animals, like people, have personalities and varying modes of behavior. Some want to be friendly; some don't. Others will listen and obey your commands; others won't. The better you know the animal, the better your chances of getting an unusual picture.

For most shots, you'll want to get as close to the animal as possible. Fill the frame with your subject. In the case of a cat or small dog, this might

ABOVE **Portrait of dogs and owner, by Elliott Erwitt (1974)**

mean kneeling or sitting on the ground. Indoors, you might try placing the camera on the floor.

Some dogs are made uneasy by the camera. It's a struggle to get them to look into the lens. Saying the dog's name can help. In any event, extra patience on your part may be required.

As the above paragraph suggests, use flash only as a last resort when taking photos of animals. The brilliant burst of light can startle them; they may get sulky. Horses can be especially skittish when made to contend with flash. If you're in a situation where you must use flash to photograph an easily-startled horse, take several pictures at some distance from the animal. Move closer in stages. The animal should eventually become accustomed to the flashes of light.

If you're a real animal enthusiast, try taking pictures at zoos and aquariums. Check in advance to find out when feeding times are scheduled. That's when animals are likely to be the most active.

ABOVE   **Cats and fishes, France, by Bruno Barbey (2006) | A dog with sunglasses on, by Martin Parr (1998)**

[A tale in pictures ...]
STORY TELLING

Many great photographers have used their camera to tell stories. **Lewis Hine**, for example, told in pictures how the Empire State Building was constructed in New York City in the early 1930s. Upon its completion in 1931, it ranked as the tallest building in the world.

Try telling a story of your own in pictures. Choose an event that will lend itself to a wide range of pictures, to indoor and outdoor shots, to close-ups and landscapes. It could be a day at the beach, a family vacation, a birthday party, or maybe a day in the life of a family member or friend.

Plan your shooting sequence in advance. You'll want your photographic story to have a **beginning, middle, and an ending**. And you'll want to get a picture or two that conveys the feeling, the flavor of the event. Try to limit the story to 6-8 pictures.

Suppose you want your story to tell of the events surrounding a day at school. Begin when you leave home and meet your friends and board the school bus. Use a long shot to show the school itself. Take a close-up of a sign or plaque bearing the school's name. Of course, you'll want a classroom shot and perhaps a full-length portrait of a teacher or two. Include pictures of any special event that takes place during the day. Lunch would be in this category. Then take a picture or two to represent the last hours of the day and the bus trip home.

For a final photo in the sequence, show how you felt about the day. Pictures that reveal emotion make good closing photos. Take a self-portrait that shows your feelings toward the day — lighthearted, bored, thoughtful ... what?

The final step is to edit your photos. Toss out any of those that don't advance the story in any way. If your series of photographs tells the story without the aid of any words of explanation, pat yourself on the back; you've done a great job.

ABOVE Photos showing the construction of the Empire State Building, by Lewis Hine (1931)

Hine's photographs showed how construction workers put up the Empire State Building "piece by piece." His images also revealed the bravery of these men, who had to perform their daily tasks while perched on narrow steel beams many hundreds of feet above the ground.

[Making pictures that trick the eye ...]
FUNNY PHOTOS

It's been said that, **"The camera always lies."** In a sense, the statement is true. Often the camera lens distorts the image you frame in your viewfinder* so as to give a twisted meaning to your picture.

These tourists are posing as if they are holding up the leaning Tower of Pisa in Pisa, Italy. Martin Parr took this picture in 1990.

!

Foreshortening is one example of this distortion. When the lens acts to foreshorten or reduce the physical distance in an image, it creates a misleading visual impression. A comical photo is often the result.

Try this: Position a friend to stand a few feet in front of you with one arm outstretched, the hand open, the palm facing upward. Looking through the viewfinder, carefully adjust the focus until the model's hand is lined up with the base of a towering building, a church steeple, a big tree, or some other tall object

Martin Parr, "Ooh La La," Holland, 1997

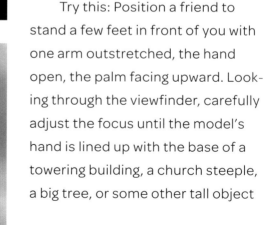

that is a good distance from the camera. Then snap the picture. The image that results will give the impression that your model is actually holding the distant subject in the palm of his hand. This is distortion by foreshortening. The camera lied.

[Making games out of your photos ...]

PUZZLER

Once you've taken a bunch of pictures and gotten them printed, what can you do with them? You can show them to your family and friends, of course, send them to distant relatives via the Internet, or put them in an album, which becomes a kind of memory book.

You can also use them as a basis for **fun projects**. You can, for example, turn a photograph into a picture puzzle. A completed puzzle makes a nice gift.

You'll need a photograph that's at least 8×10 inches (20×25 centimeters) in size. You'll also need a piece of heavy white cardboard that's the same size, and some glue. Glue the photo to the cardboard. Once the glue is dry, turn the cardboard over and draw lines dividing it into puzzle pieces.

The final step is to cut the cardboard into pieces following the lines you've drawn. Use a scissors. For really heavy cardboard, use an X-Acto knife.

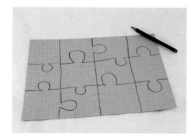

Panoramic photos make the best puzzles. Take a picture of the trees in a thickly grown forest or the rolling surf at an ocean beach.

Decide in advance how challenging you want the puzzle to be. The smaller you cut the pieces, the harder the puzzle.

Photographic picture puzzles are often called photocollages. They're a specialty British artist David Hockney. Some of Hockney's photocollages have become well known. In *Pearlblossom Highway*, Hockney took pieces of photos from a road trip and arranged them so as to create a desert scene, but one with strange overtones.

!

[Mixing images and words ...]

SIGNING UP

You can use your camera and a little ingenuity to create your own **photographic sign**. This project will send you out into your neighborhood to take photos of the letters of the alphabet. Your mission is to search for the letters that make up your name, and then use them to make a placard or sign that you can use for public display.

Photographer **Walker Evans** was fascinated by the letters and words on street signs. For him, signs were an important part of American culture. Sometimes Evans would show how signs could "take over" a city street. In one such photo, the advertising signs on a building and truck seem to blend together, making the building and truck look almost like one object.

Photograph letters on billboards or those that appear on the sides of trucks. You'll want close-up photos; fill the frame with each letter.

You can also photograph pieces of metal, wood, or plastic that **represent the letters** you're seeking. For example, a fencepost or slim tree trunk can stand for the letter I. A bicycle wheel or the rim of a wastebasket can be the letter O.

If you're unable to find a particular letter that you need, write the letter on the sidewalk in chalk, then photograph it.

Once you've photographed all the letters you need and have printed each one, paste them in proper order on a piece of stiff cardboard. You might want to add a photo or two of yourself to the display.

[**Check out a world of photographic tools online.**]

EDITING YOUR PICTURES

Once you've downloaded your photos into your computer, you've opened the door to a world of picture magic. Thanks to software that has been especially designed for digital cameras, you can improve your pictures, change them, and combine them with other images in ways that will please and surprise you.

Your digital camera may be equipped with software that enables you to do some of the things described in this chapter. But whether or not your camera offers these features, it's a good idea to become familiar with the free editing software available on the Internet. Such programs perform the basic editing tasks described in the paragraphs that follow.

It's easy to get a rundown of software sites. Search the Internet for the "best digital photographic editor for kids" or "free photo editing software for kids." Then pick out the programs that appeal to you. Free photo editing software will permit you to perform these tasks:

Cropping

When you crop a picture, you trim it so as to eliminate anything you don't want. For example, when you crop the edges of the picture, you call attention to the main subject. You make the picture more dramatic. You can also use cropping to get rid of a cluttered background or objects in the foreground that distract you from the main subject.

Straightening

You can straighten any photo that is askew. All you have to do is align it against the viewfinder's boxed grid.

Brightness and Contrast*

If a photograph from your camera disappoints you because it is too bright or too dark, don't worry. You can brighten or darken it with brightness control.

You can also improve the tonal quality by increasing or decreasing the picture's contrast. If the shadows are too bright, you can make them darker. If the highlights are too dark, you can lighten them. Boosting the tonal quality of a picture can even correct a slight blurring problem.

Dodging* and Burning*

In some pictures, you'll see a need to lighten or darken a particular area. You do this with the dodge and burn tool. Dodging allows you to lighten an area; burning enables you to darken it.

Redeye

Often in photographs of faces, the pupils of the eyes will appear red. In some software packages, the redeye function quickly detects this problem and automatically corrects it. With other types of software, you click a reset button and then drag the mouse around each affected eye in order to make the correction.

Incidentally, such software gets rid of only the color red. It doesn't correct eyes that appear yellow, green, or white because of flash problems.

Retouching

You use the retouch tool to remove isolated spots or stains, even disfigurement that might appear in a portrait photo. Old photos that have stains or cracks can be restored.

Text

One click of the text tool allows you to insert a block of your own written material anywhere on your photo. You can just type it in, selecting the size and style you want.

[More photo fun on your computer ...]
PLAYING WITH PICTURES

Basic editing is just the beginning. Other online resources enable you to create countless weird and wacky things with your photographs. Using an Internet search engine, go to one of the many websites that list the free picture-editing sites that focus on fun. There are hundreds of them.

These sites allow you to:

- make multiple pictures of the same image on a single piece of paper
- make fancy cards, gift tags, calendars, personalized stationery, bookplates, and birthday party invitations
- create your own personalized dollar bill or playing cards
- make your own face (or someone else's) look silly or even moronic
- try on celebrity hair and makeup
- put your own face on a magazine cover

For even greater power in photo editing, professional photographers and graphic artists turn to advanced software. These programs have sophisticated features not available in free programs. Such programs can be expensive, however.

German artist Andreas Gursky uses both cameras and computers to make his unique photographs. Gursky's vast landscapes are actually many different photos of the same scene. They have been blended together through the use of sophisticated photo-editing software. Gursky's wizardry enables him to show extended views of a particular area. His image of Rimini, Italy, for example, depicts a huge section of the city's beaches and coastline.

GLOSSARY

aperture — The lens opening that admits light into the camera.

available light — The light that is present without the use of flash or flood lamps.

burning — An editing tool that allows you to darken a particular area of a photo.

contrast — The amount of difference between light and dark tones in a photograph.

composition — The art of arranging a photograph's various elements — the subject, foreground, and background — so as to achieve a unified whole.

depth of field — The area of a photograph that is in focus.

dodging — An editing tool that allows you to lighten a particular area of a photo.

dpi — Dots per inch—the measure of resolution (or sharpness) in a photograph.

exposure — The amount of light required to produce a photographic image.

focal length — The distance from the camera to the object being photographed. Also called focal distance.

f. stop	A number that indicates the size of the lens opening. The higher the f. number, the smaller the lens opening.
ISO number	A number that indicates how sensitive a camera is to the amount of light present. The higher the ISO rating, the faster the shutter speed. (ISO stands for International Standardization Organization.)
pixel	The smallest element of a digital image that can be processed.
ppi	Pixels per inch.
resolution	The degree of sharpness in a photo, often expressed in pixels per inch.
shutter	A mechanical device for opening and closing the aperture of the lens to allow the exposure to be made.
viewfinder	A camera feature that enables the user to determine what will appear in the photograph.
white balance	The tonal quality of a picture. (Digital cameras offer a white balance selection to match the available light source.)

Acknowledgments

Special thanks are due Kay O'Reilly for her diligence and expertise in revising and correcting the manuscript in its various stages, Marie Phelan for her unmatched skills as a computer guru, and Odile Kory for enlisting support from her European sources.

George Sullivan · New York City

Imprint

© Prestel Verlag, Munich · London · New York, 2011
© for the works held by the artists or their legal heirs except for: ©Edward Burtynsky, courtesy Stefan Röpke, Cologne and Nicholas Metivier, Toronto; Bruno Barbey, Henri Cartier-Bresson, Elliott Erwitt, Martine Franck, Philippe Halsman, Steve McCurry and Martin Parr: Magnum Photos/Agentur Focus; Andreas Gursky and Alexander Rodchenko: VG Bild-Kunst, Bonn 2011; August Sander ©Die Photographische Sammlung/SK Stiftung Kultur – August Sander Archiv, Köln/VG Bild-Kunst, Bonn 2011; Photomosaic® ©Robert Silvers, www.photomosaic.com

Picture credits: p. 68 top: Bruno Barbey/Magnum Photos/Agentur Focus; p. 52, p. 76, p. 79 bottom: Boris Bergmann; p. 74, p. 80 top, p. 82 top: Boris Bergmann, courtesy Tierpark Hellabrunn, Munich; p. 30/31: Henri Cartier-Bresson/Magnum Photos/Agentur Focus; p. 66, p. 67: Elliott Erwitt/Magnum Photos/Agentur Focus; p. 58: Martine Franck/Magnum Photos/Agentur Focus; p. 84: Andreas Gursky/Courtesy Sprüth Magers Berlin London; p. 53 top: Philippe Halsman/Magnum Photos/Agentur Focus; p. 65: Nigel Hicks/National Geographic Stock; p. 39: Lewis Hine/ullstein bild; p. 79 top, p. 80 bottom, p. 82 bottom: Nele Krüger; p. 68 bottom: Doris Kutschbach; p. 50, p. 83: Aime LaMontagne; p. 54: Steve McCurry/Magnum Photos/Agentur Focus; p. 64: National Geographic Stock/Alaska Stock Images; p. 68 Mitte, p. 72 bottom, p. 73: Martin Parr/Magnum Photos/Agentur Focus; p. 51: Clive Rose/Getty Images; p. 57: August Sander/Die Photographische Sammlung/SK Stiftung Kultur – August Sander Archiv, Köln; p. 75: Richard Schmidt

Prestel, a member of Verlagsgruppe Random House GmbH

Prestel Verlag, Munich
www.prestel.de

Prestel Publishing Ltd.
4 Bloomsbury Place
London WC1A 2QA

Prestel Publishing
900 Broadway, Suite 603
New York, NY 10003

www.prestel.com

Library of Congress Control Number is available; British Library Cataloguing-in-Publication Data: a catalogue record for this book is available from the British Library; Deutsche Nationalbibliothek holds a record of this publication in the Deutsche National-bibliografie; detailed bibliographical data can be found under: http://dnb.ddb.de

Prestel books are available worldwide. Please contact your nearest bookseller or one of the above addresses for information concerning your local distributor.

Edited/Copyedited by: Brad Finger
Project Management: Andrea Jaroni
Picture Editor: Andrea Jaroni
Design and layout:
SOFAROBOTNIK, Augsburg & Munich
Production: Nele Krüger
Art direction: Cilly Klotz
Origination: Reproline Genceller, Munich
Printing and Binding: Neografia, Martin

Verlagsgruppe Random House FSC®-DEU-0100
The FSC-certified paper *Hello Fat Matt* has been supplied by Condat, Le Lardin Saint-Lazare, France.

ISBN 978-3-7913-7079-8